SCHOLASTIC
TRUE OR FALSE

Baby Animals

BY MELVIN AND GILDA BERGER

ISBN-13: 978-0-545-00391-9
ISBN-10: 0-545-00391-1

10 9 8 7 6 5 4 3 2   08 09 10 11 12

Printed in the U.S.A.   23
First printing, February 2008
Book design by Nancy Sabato

A baby horse is called a pony. TRUE OR FALSE?

FALSE!

A baby horse is called a foal. (A pony is a small kind of horse.)

Most female horses (mares) give birth to only one foal at a time. The foal's legs seem very long for its body. But as it gets older, the legs grow more slowly than the rest of the animal's body. A young male horse less than four years old is called a colt. A young female horse under age four is called a filly.

A horse's "foot" is really just one large toe covered by a hard hoof!

Baby frogs
look like
their moms
and dads.

TRUE
OR
FALSE?

FALSE! Baby frogs look like fish, not like grown-up frogs.

Frogs start life when a female lays eggs in water. After a male fertilizes the eggs, they hatch into tiny tadpoles with long tails and gills for breathing underwater. About six weeks later, the tadpoles grow legs and their tails get smaller. They develop lungs, so they can breathe air. By sixteen weeks, the tadpoles move out of the water as frogs! Most frogs live on land and in water.

A female frog may lay thousands of eggs at a time!

Mother alligators take good care of their babies. TRUE OR FALSE?

TRUE! Some female alligators carry their babies to safe hiding places.

A female alligator lays ten to fifty eggs at a time. The babies hatch from eggs, just like baby birds. Each baby, called a hatchling, is about as long as a pencil! Sometimes the mother carries the hatchlings in her mouth to safety near a river or a lake. Few animals would try to steal a young alligator from this mother's jaw!

Baby alligators go off on their own before they are three years old!

Deer babies keep their spots for life. TRUE OR FALSE?

FALSE! Most deer babies, or fawns, lose their spots between three and five months of age.

The white spots help to hide the fawn. A female deer (doe) usually gives birth to twins; sometimes she has a single baby or triplets. The babies are born in a hidden spot, away from other deer. When they can walk, the fawns follow their mother to the field or forest. The mother is always alert to the danger of attack from enemies—animal or human.

Only male deer (bucks) grow antlers.

Sea turtle babies never see their parents. **TRUE** OR **FALSE?**

TRUE! Female sea turtles lay eggs on a beach and crawl back into the sea before their babies are born.

The sun warms the eggs, and the baby sea turtles break out of their shells. Quickly, the newborns race down to the sea. They flee the birds, dogs, crabs, or even humans that prey on them. Once in the water, however, the baby sea turtles are quite safe. They can swim faster than the fastest human swimmers!

Female sea turtles lay their eggs on the same beaches where they were born.

Polar bears are born in the spring. **TRUE OR FALSE?**

FALSE! Polar bear babies are born in the winter.

A polar bear mother digs a den in the snow. Here she gives birth to two cubs. The mother feeds the cubs milk from her body. As soon as it is spring, the mother and her cubs leave the den. The mother teaches her young how to hunt for seals, which polar bears love to eat. After about two years, the cubs leave to live on their own.

Polar bear cubs learn to catch seals through holes in the ice.

Only the mother robin feeds the babies. **TRUE OR FALSE?**

FALSE! Mother and father robins take turns feeding the babies.

Female robins lay their blue eggs in nests built of twigs, mud, and grass. Sometimes, the father robin helps. The mother sits on the eggs for about two weeks until the eggs hatch. Both the mother and father find food for their hungry babies. Robins eat fruits, berries, earthworms, and insects like caterpillars and grasshoppers.

Three to five baby robins hatch at one time.

whales can breathe underwater. TRUE OR FALSE?

FALSE! whales breathe air.

Whales are mammals and like all mammals, they breathe air. A baby whale, or calf, is born alive in the water. As soon as it's born, the mother whale lifts her calf to the surface for its first breath. The calf breathes in and out through a blowhole on the top of its head. Underwater, the whale's blowhole is shut tight. When the whale surfaces, it breathes out fast. The "blow" looks like a very high fountain mist or spray.

whales can hold their breath underwater as long as two hours!

Emperor penguin dads keep the eggs warm. **TRUE OR FALSE?**

TRUE!

After the female lays an egg, the penguin dad takes over. Penguins live in the water, but mothers lay their eggs on land or ice. The female transfers the egg to the top of her mate's feet, then goes to sea to feed. The dad keeps the egg warm under a flap of his belly. The mother returns weeks later, usually just before the egg is ready to hatch, to relieve the male, so he can feed. If the egg hatches before the mom returns, the dad can feed the baby penguin (chick) a milky substance from his throat.

Penguins are birds that swim—but can't fly!

Newborn kittens cannot see or hear. **TRUE OR FALSE?**

TRUE! It takes about two weeks for a kitten's eyes and ears to open.

A mother cat takes good care of her kittens. She chooses a dark, warm, and quiet place to bear her young, so they won't be bothered or harmed by enemies. Also, the dark place helps protect the kittens' sensitive eyes from injury by bright lights. The mother cat cuddles her babies and cleans them with her tongue.

The father cat does not take care of the kittens at all.

Puppies can walk as soon as they are born. TRUE OR FALSE?

FALSE! A puppy learns to walk when it is about three weeks old.

Newborn puppies cannot see, hear, or even move around. They mostly sleep and drink milk from their mother. In about two to three weeks, their eyes are open and they start to walk. As soon as they have their first teeth, they are ready to eat solid food. A group of puppies born at the same time is called a litter.

Dogs live an average of thirteen years, which equals about seventy years for a human.

Baby lions are called kittens. TRUE OR FALSE?

FALSE! Baby lions are called cubs.

Lion cubs live in family groups called prides. The male lion rarely helps the female lions (lionesses) care for the cubs. His job is to frighten away enemies and protect the pride. The male also leaves most of the hunting to the lionesses. The lionesses teach the young lions how to hunt.

A pride of lions usually includes at least one male and two or three lionesses with their cubs.

Brown bear cubs are born with brown fur. **TRUE OR FALSE?**

FALSE! Newborn brown bear cubs have almost no fur.

At birth, brown bear cubs just have a fuzz of hair or fur. As they grow, though, the hair becomes very long and shaggy and takes on its own color. The fur of full-grown brown bears ranges from a light cream to nearly black. But whatever the color, the thick fur makes the bears look even bigger—and scarier—than they really are.

The teddy bear is named after a bear that President Theodore (or Teddy) Roosevelt would not shoot.

Baby wolves are called pups. TRUE OR FALSE?

TRUE! Like dogs, baby wolves are called pups, short for puppies.

In early summer, a mother wolf gives birth in an underground den to as many as six pups. Wolf pups live in family groups called packs. All of the members of a pack help care for the pups. The pups play-fight from an early age. This kind of play gets them ready for real fights and successful hunting when they grow up.

Most packs have a dozen or more wolves that can include a mom and dad, pups, and aunts and uncles!

Sea otter babies cry like human babies. **TRUE OR FALSE?**

TRUE!

A sea otter baby, or pup, stays with its mother for up to eight months. During that time, the mother frequently dives to the ocean bottom for food, such as crabs, mussels, sea urchins, snails, starfish, squid, and some kinds of fish. When feeding her baby, the mother floats on her back. Her belly forms a kind of crib for the baby and a table for eating.

A newborn sea otter pup is so light that it floats on the surface like a cork!

Baby goats learn to butt heads at an early age. **TRUE** OR **FALSE?**

TRUE! Butting heads helps young goats settle fights.

Until it is one year old, a baby goat is called a kid. The dad is a buck (or billy goat); the mom is a doe (or nanny goat). As the kids grow older, they play and fight. Butting heads and pushing against one another help them choose their leaders. Goats grow up to have different colors, from white to red to black.

Goats mostly eat grass, but they will nibble almost anything.

All baby
kangaroos
have the same
name—billy. **TRUE OR FALSE?**

FALSE! Baby kangaroos are all called joeys, though no one knows where the name came from.

At birth, a joey is about the size of a bean. As soon as it is born, it crawls inside a special pouch on its mother's belly. The pouch is like a large pocket. Here it drinks its mother's milk and grows bigger and bigger. After about nine months, the joey climbs out and hops around. But if frightened or hungry, it jumps right back in.

A joey in danger will ride in the pouch, since adult kangaroos can hop faster than most people can run!

A baby elephant sucks on its trunk like a human baby sucks its thumb.

TRUE
OR
FALSE?

TRUE! A baby elephant uses its trunk for sucking—as well as for smelling, spraying water, inhaling, and carrying branches.

A baby elephant is called a calf. Its mother joins other females in the herd to take very good care of *all* the calves. They protect the calves from lions, tigers, and hyenas. The calves play with other young elephants and seem to enjoy splashing water and rolling in dirt or mud. A calf usually stays with its mother for up to sixteen years.

Elephants care for their babies longer than any other animal—except humans.

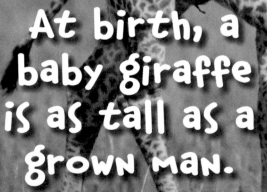

At birth, a baby giraffe is as tall as a grown man.

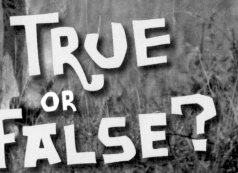

TRUE OR FALSE?

TRUE! A newborn giraffe is about six feet tall!

A baby giraffe is called a calf—just like a baby cow. A few weeks after its birth, the giraffe calf joins a small group of other calves. The group is like a nursery, with the mothers taking turns caring for the youngsters. Each mom feeds milk to her calf often during the day. After about a year in the nursery, the giraffe can care for itself.

A baby giraffe has the same number of neck bones as humans do—except that its bones are much, much longer!

Baby tigers purr like kittens. TRUE OR FALSE?

TRUE!

Baby tigers purr, but adult tigers do not!

Tiger cubs grow into the biggest of the big cats—and become among the most feared of all animals. When the cubs are about two months old, their mother catches and kills animals for them to eat. She also teaches them how to hunt. By eighteen months of age, the young tigers can find food for themselves. Some stay with their mothers for up to thirty months.

A mother tiger kills sixty to seventy prey—usually deer and wild boars—a year to feed herself and her cubs.

Baby dolphins cannot get sunburned. TRUE OR FALSE?

FALSE! If dolphin babies spend too much time on the surface of the water, they get sunburned.

All dolphins have smooth, thin, hairless skin—much like the surface of a balloon. Too much sunshine can easily harm their very delicate outer covering. As dolphins swim, tiny flakes wash off their skin, keeping their bodies very smooth. Small wonder that dolphins can streak through water at superfast speeds.

Dolphins get a new outer skin every two hours.

Young gorillas
live with
their families
forever. TRUE OR FALSE?

FALSE! Most young gorillas leave their families between the ages of seven and ten.

A gorilla baby stays with its mother day and night for about four to six years. At first, the mother carries the baby around in her arms. After about four months, the baby can grasp its mother's hair to ride on her back. A few months later, the baby can walk by itself and travels alongside the adult members of the family group.

Young gorillas may burp loudly when they finish a meal!

Index

J. Rogers School

DATE DUE

APR 6 2010	
APR 7 2010	
MAY 27 2010	
MAY 27 2010	
MAY 27 2010	
OCT 13 2010	
NOV 30 2010	

38-2931

SCHOLASTIC

TRUE

Baby Animals

TRUE OR FALSE?

Are polar bears born in the Spring?

Can newborn kittens see or hear?

Can baby dolphins get Sunburned?

Scholastic True or False
is a young Science series in a fun
question-and-answer format. Each
book contains 22 true-or-false questions
with a photograph on every page. Read
the question on the right and turn
the page to see the answer on
the left!

$4.99 US / $5.99 CA

ISBN-13: 978-0-545-00391
ISBN-10: 0-545-00391-1

SCHOLASTIC

www.scholastic.com

EAN   9 780545 003919